BLAZERS

Wild Outdoors

Bowhunting

by Thomas K. Adamson

Reading Consultant: Barbara J. Fox
Reading Specialist
North Carolina State University

Content Consultant: Greg Slone
Next Generation Hunting
Bowling Green, Kentucky

CAPSTONE PRESS
a capstone imprint

Blazers is published by Capstone Press,
151 Good Counsel Drive, P.O. Box 669, Mankato, Minnesota 56002.
www.capstonepub.com

Books published by Capstone Press are manufactured with paper
containing at least 10 percent post-consumer waste.

Library of Congress Cataloging-in-Publication Data
Adamson, Thomas K., 1970–
Bowhunting / by Thomas K. Adamson.
p. cm.— (Blazers. Wild outdoors)
Includes bibliographical references and index.
Summary: "Describes the equipment, techniques, and safety skills needed for bowhunting"—
Provided by publisher.
ISBN 978-1-4296-4808-0 (library binding)
1. Bowhunting—Juvenile literature. I. Title. II. Series.
SK36.A33 2011
799.2'15—dc22   2009053410

Editorial Credits

Christine Peterson, editor; Veronica Correia, designer; Sarah Schuette, photo stylist;
    Marcy Morin, scheduler; Laura Manthe, production specialist

Photo Credits

Capstone Studio/Karon Dubke, all photos except:
Newscom/MCT/Kansas CityStar/Brent Frazee, 29

Artistic Effects

Capstone Press/Karon Dubke (woods); Shutterstock: rvika (wood), rvrspb (fence), VikaSuh (sign)

Printed in the United States of America in Stevens Point, Wisconsin.
092010
005957R

Table of Contents

Chapter 1

On the Hunt!

You've spent weeks scouting the perfect hunting area. You've practiced your shooting skills. Now you wait silently in the woods, watching a huge **buck**.

buck—a male deer

Wild Fact:

Bowhunters hunt for deer, wild turkeys, elk, and antelope. Some hunters even bowhunt for bears.

Wild Fact:

Hunters make sure they have a clear shot at an animal. That way they kill the animal instead of wounding it.

Finally, you get a clear shot at the deer. You slowly pull back the bowstring and squeeze the **release** trigger. The arrow launches silently and hits its mark. You just landed a huge buck.

release—a device that holds the string; hunters squeeze a trigger on the release to shoot the arrow

Chapter 2

Be Prepared!

A successful hunt begins with the right bow. Most bowhunters use a **compound bow**. These bows are more accurate than traditional bows. Pulleys on a compound bow make it easier to pull back the string.

compound bow—a bow that uses pulleys to make it easier for the hunter to pull back the string

pulleys

compound bow

Wild Fact:

Traditional bows are the longbow and recurve.

Arrows fly through the air at more than 200 feet (61 meters) per second. Most arrows are made of aluminum, carbon, or both. Arrow tips are made of steel. **Broadhead tips** are most popular.

broadhead tips

broadhead tip—a steel arrow tip with three blades that stick out

Wild Fact:

Many states require hunters to pass a bowhunter education class.

Bowhunters also need other gear. An arm guard protects the forearm. A release helps a hunter shoot more accurately. Hunters use calls to attract some prey.

arm guard

release

practice target

Wild Fact:

Bowhunters practice their shooting skills by firing at targets. Some targets look like animals.

call

treestand

blinds

binoculars

target

face mask

harness

string silencer

camouflage paint

4

Bowhunting Equipment

compound bow

camouflage clothing

scents

arrow rest

arrows

arm guard

Chapter 3

Skills and Techniques

Bowhunters want to be invisible to animals. They wear **camouflage** clothing to blend into their surroundings. Hunters cover their faces with masks or face paint.

camouflage—coloring that helps hunters blend in with their surroundings

Wild Fact:

Bowhunters don't always wear camouflage. Some just wear natural colors like brown and green.

Animals can smell people from a long way off. Hunters hide their **scents** with special soaps and sprays. They stay **downwind** of animals. The wind carries hunters' scents away from animals.

animal scent

SCENT

scent—an odor
downwind—to be in the same direction as the wind is blowing

Wild Fact:

Animals can smell your breath too. Some hunters chew odorless gum.

Hunters spot prey from treestands and **blinds**. Most stands are 15 feet (4.6 meters) above ground. Hunters get a wide view of their hunting area in stands. On the ground, blinds keep hunters hidden.

blind—a covering that helps bowhunters hide from animals

Some bowhunters **stalk** animals. Stalking takes patience. Hunters walk slowly and quietly when following animals. If a hunter moves quickly, the animal will run away.

stalk—to follow an animal as quietly as possible

Wild Fact:

Bowhunters get as close as 20 yards (18 meters) to the animal before shooting.

Chapter 4

Safety

Bowhunters know the importance of safety. Hunters cover sharp arrows when they are not hunting. They aim only at targets they plan to shoot. They make sure the target is an animal and not another person.

Wild Fact:

Hunters make sure their arrows and bow are not damaged before using them.

Hunters use **harnesses** so they don't fall out of treestands. They climb into their stands without their equipment. They use rope to pull up the bows and arrows.

harness

harness—straps that keep a hunter from falling off the treestand

Chapter 5

Take On the Challenge!

Bowhunters never forget the thrill of a successful hunt. Their patience and skill pay off when they bag their prey. Are you ready for the challenge of bowhunting?

Wild Fact:

All states require hunters to buy some type of hunting license.

Glossary

accurate (AK-yuh-ruht)—able to hit the target at which a hunter aimed

aluminum (uh-LOO-muh-nuhm)—a lightweight, silver-colored metal

blind (BLYND)—a hidden place from which hunters can shoot prey

broadhead tip (BRAWD-hed TIP)—a flat arrowhead shaped like a triangle with sharp edges

buck (BUHK)—a male deer

camouflage (KA-muh-flahzh)—coloring that makes hunters blend in with their surroundings

compound bow (KOM-pound BOH)—a bow that uses pulleys to make it easier for the hunter to pull back the string

downwind (DOUN-wind)—to be in the same direction as the wind is blowing

harness (HAR-niss)—a device that straps one thing to another; harness straps keep hunters from falling off their treestands

pulley (PUL-ee)—a grooved wheel turned by a rope, belt, or chain that often moves heavy objects

release (ri-LEESS)—a device that holds the string; hunters squeeze a trigger on the release to shoot the arrow

scent (SENT)—the odor of a person or animal

stalk (STAWK)—to hunt or track an animal as quietly as possible

Read More

Adamson, Thomas K. *Deer Hunting.* Wild Outdoors. Mankato, Minn.: Capstone Press, 2011.

Gunderson, Jessica. *Bowhunting for Fun!* For Fun! Minneapolis: Compass Point Books, 2009.

Lewis, Joan. *Hunting.* Get Going! Hobbies. Chicago: Heinemann Library, 2006.

Weintraub, Aileen. *Bowhunting.* The Great Outdoors. Mankato, Minn.: Capstone Press, 2008.

Internet Sites

FactHound offers a safe, fun way to find Internet sites related to this book. All of the sites on FactHound have been researched by our staff.

Here's all you do:

Visit *www.facthound.com*

Type in this code: **9781429648080**

Index

DATE DUE